HOW-TO LIBRARY

CRAFTING WITH TISSUE PAPER

Written and Illustrated by Kathleen Petelinsek

CHERRY LAKE PUBLISHING • ANN ARBOR, MICHIGAN

Published in the United States of America by Cherry Lake Publishing
Ann Arbor, Michigan
www.cherrylakepublishing.com

Photo Credits: Page 4, ©Fotyma/Shutterstock.com; page 5, ©AN NGUYEN/Shutterstock.com; page 6, ©Ignia Andrei/Shutterstock.com.

Library of Congress Cataloging-in-Publication Data
Petelinsek, Kathleen, author.
  Crafting with tissue paper / by Kathleen Petelinsek.
    pages cm. — (Crafts) (How-to library)
  Summary: "Learn how to create a variety of fun craft projects using tissue paper"—Provided by publisher.
  Audience: Grades 4 to 6.
  Includes bibliographical references and index.
  ISBN 978-1-63137-779-2 (lib. bdg.) — ISBN 978-1-63137-799-0 (pbk.) — ISBN 978-1-63137-839-3 (e-book) — ISBN 978-1-63137-819-5 (pdf)
  1. Paper work—Juvenile literature. 2. Tissue paper—Juvenile literature. 3. Handicraft—Juvenile literature. I. Title.

TT870.P472 2014
745.54—dc23   2014003300

Cherry Lake Publishing would like to acknowledge the work of The Partnership for 21st Century Skills. Please visit www.p21.org for more information.

Printed in the United States of America
Corporate Graphics Inc.
July 2014

TABLE OF CONTENTS

It Began as Toilet Tissue

Today, tissue paper is available in almost any color you can imagine.

In 1857, the world was introduced to toilet tissue, a paper product invented by Joseph Gayetty. Gayetty's paper was different than other papers of the time. It was also different from the toilet paper of today. It did not come on rolls. Instead, it was packaged as individual, flat, thin sheets of paper.

In 1863, a **tailor** named Ebenezer Butterick realized that the thin toilet tissue paper could be used to make sewing patterns. His patterns quickly caught on among people who wanted to make their own clothing at home. It didn't take long for people to find other uses for toilet tissue. Some even used it to wrap gifts!

In the early 20th century, it was still common for gifts to be wrapped in white or brown tissue paper that closely resembled toilet tissue. But by 1917, a store owned by the Hall brothers began selling red, green, and even patterned tissue paper as gift wrap. The paper was so popular that the brothers ran out of it. They began offering a thicker colored paper at 10 cents a sheet. The paper sold so quickly that they increased the price to 25 cents the following year. Once again, it sold out. The Hall brothers soon founded a company called Hallmark to specialize in selling gift wrap. At the time, the brothers had no idea they were launching an entire **industry**.

Tissue paper is still used to wrap gifts today.

Decorating with Tissue Paper

Tissue paper's bright colors and thinness make it perfect for many craft projects.

Today, tissue paper is primarily used as gift wrap. However, its qualities also make it very useful for creating craft projects. Tissue paper is available in many colors and patterns. It is so thin that it is almost **translucent**. It also bleeds when it gets wet, creating a tie-dye effect. Today's tissue paper is made from recycled paper pulp. This means trees are not cut down to create it. It is very affordable, and most people have some at home. This makes it the perfect crafting material!

To begin crafting with tissue paper, you will need to gather a few basic supplies. Put them in a box or plastic tub to keep them together. This will make them easy to find when you want to work with them. Below is a list of materials to gather:

- Tissue paper in a variety of colors and patterns
- Scissors
- Glue
- Pipe cleaners
- Construction paper
- Paintbrushes
- Ruler
- Sketch paper
- Needle and thread

As you work through this book, check the instructions for each project to see if there are other supplies you need before you begin working. Have fun!

Skills and Terms

Before we get started, there are a few skills and terms that you will need to know in order to complete the projects in this book.

Accordion fold: If you have ever made a paper fan, this is the same fold. Begin with your paper lying flat in front of you. Fold the edge nearest to you up. Turn the paper over and fold the folded edge up. The second fold should be the same width as the first fold. Turn the paper over again and fold the folded edge up. Continue turning and folding until the paper is folded all the way to the end.

Double-threaded needle: Stick one end of the thread through your needle and pull it all the way through the eye until it meets back up with the other end. Tie the two ends together in a knot.

Decoupage: Decoupage is the art of gluing paper to an object. The crafts in this book use tissue paper. However, you can use magazine pages, wrapping paper, or even newspaper to decoupage an object. Any paper works. Here are instructions for using tissue paper and glue or polycrylic:

Materials

- Old newspapers
- Tissue paper
- Scissors
- Glue or polycrylic
- Bowl
- 1-inch (2.5 cm) paintbrush
- Item to decoupage

Steps

1. Spread newspapers out to protect your work surface.
2. Cut the tissue paper into small pieces.
3. Pour some glue or polycrylic into the bowl. Dip the paintbrush into the glue. Brush a spot of glue or polycrylic onto the item you wish to decoupage.
4. Place the tissue paper on the glue or polycrylic spot.
5. Brush over the top of the tissue paper with more glue or polycrylic.
6. Continue to add tissue paper until the item is covered.

Hawaiian Lei

This is a great party craft. Host a Hawaiian-themed party and ask your guests to dress in summer clothes and flip-flops. Everyone can make their own lei!

Materials
- Tissue paper (different colors)
- Scissors
- Ruler
- Needle and thread

Steps
1. Cut 20 strips of different colored tissue paper into rectangles that measure 3 x 20 inches (8 x 51 cm).
2. Cut a piece of thread that is 4 feet (1.2 m) long. Use it to double thread your needle. Your thread should now be 2 feet (61 cm) long.
3. Accordion fold each piece of tissue paper, one at a time. Each fold should be 3 inches (8 cm) deep. When you are done, each piece of

tissue paper will be folded
into a 3-inch (8 cm) square.

4. Thread your needle
through the center of one of the
accordion-folded squares. Pull the
folded square toward the knot at the
end of the thread.

5. String another folded square onto
your thread in the same way. Use a
different color this time. Continue to
do this with all of your tissue paper
strips. Do not crunch them together
tightly. Instead, spread them evenly
over the length of the thread.

6. Once all of your tissue paper is
threaded, cut the needle loose from
the end of the thread. Tie the loose
ends of the thread to the knotted
end to create a loop.

7. To make the tissue look like
flowers, crumple the folded paper
squares. Gently pull the paper
apart as you crumple each piece.
Continue all the way around
the lei.

Wall Art

Use decoupage to create a unique, colorful piece of art that you can hang up on the wall.

Materials

- Tissue paper (different colors)
- Scissors
- Ruler
- Pencil
- White paper (8½ x 11 inches, or 22 x 28 cm)
- Old newspapers
- Glue
- Bowl
- Paintbrush (1 inch, or 2.5 cm)
- White poster board (8½ x 11 inches, or 22 x 28 cm)
- Frame (8½ x 11 inches, or 22 x 28 cm)

Steps

1. Cut the tissue paper into shapes that are roughly 1 inch by 1 inch (2.5 cm by 2.5 cm). You can cut squares or other shapes such as circles or rectangles.

2. Think of a simple shape. It might be your initial, an animal shape, or a heart. You could even trace your hand. Use a pencil to draw the shape on white paper.

3. Spread newspaper out to protect your work surface.

4. Pour some glue into the bowl. Use the paintbrush to decoupage the tissue paper shapes to the shape you drew on the white paper. Don't worry too much about staying within the lines. Set the paper aside to dry when you are done.

5. Once the paper is dry, cut out your shape. You should be able to see your pencil lines through the decoupage.

6. Add a thin, even layer of glue to the back side of your cutout shape.

7. Glue your artwork to the poster board.

8. Frame your artwork.

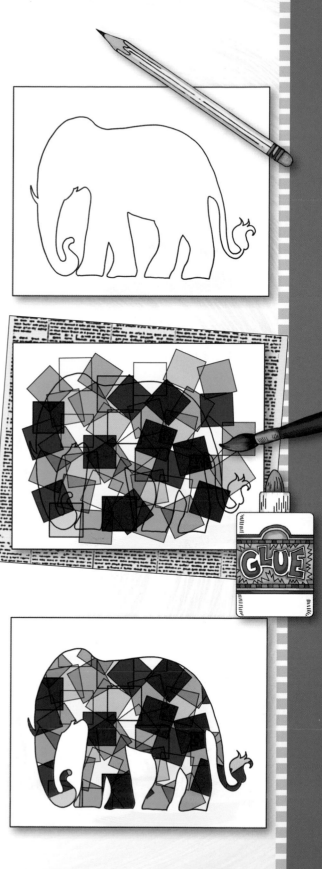

Tissue Paper Monster Puppet

Create a weird, wild puppet using tissue paper and other basic craft supplies. Make several different puppets and use them to put on a show!

Materials

- Old newspapers
- Green tissue paper
- Scissors
- Ruler
- White construction paper
- Paper lunch bag or small brown paper grocery bag
- Glue
- Black construction paper
- Paper plate
- Pencil

Steps

1. Spread newspapers out to protect your work surface.
2. Cut the green tissue paper into 1-inch (2.5 cm) squares. You will need a lot of squares (between 300 and 500, depending on the size of your paper bag). If you do not cut enough at first, you can always go back and cut more.

3. Cut two circles with a 2-inch (5 cm) **diameter** from the white construction paper.

4. Place the paper bag in front of you with the folded bottom portion of the bag on top and facing up.

5. Glue the two white circles to the top of the bag. Half of the circle should be above the edge of the bag.

6. Cut two circles with a 1-inch (2.5 cm) diameter from the black construction paper.

7. Glue the two black circles in the center of the white circles. Your puppet now has eyes! Let's give him a mouth.

8. Cut two fang shapes from the white construction paper.

9. Open the flap of the bag and glue the fangs to the bottom side.

10. Now it is time to give the monster fur. Squirt some glue onto your paper plate.

11. Place the eraser end of the pencil in the center of one of the green tissue squares. Crinkle the paper around the end of the pencil. Holding the pencil and tissue at the same time, dip the tissue paper into the glue.

12. Stick the gluey paper to the paper bag. Continue sticking the green tissue squares to the bag until all but the underside of the flap is covered. The back, front, sides, and bottom of the bag should all be covered. You will need to open the bag to do this.

13. Once the glue is dry, put your hand inside the puppet and make the monster come alive!

Tissue Paper Doll

Paper can even be used to build fun toys. Create a doll that looks exactly the way you want it to!

Materials

- Scrap paper (8½ x 11 inches, or 22 x 28 cm)
- Tissue paper (different colors)
- Pipe cleaners
- Scissors
- Ruler
- Glue
- 2 sequins or 2 googly eyes
- Black marker

Steps

1. Crumple the scrap paper into a tight ball.
2. Lay two full-size pieces of tissue paper flat on the table, one on top of the other. Cut the two pieces into large circles by cutting off the corners.
3. Place the crumpled ball in the center of the stacked tissue paper circles.

4. Gather the tissue paper up around the crumpled ball. Twist the center of a pipe cleaner around the gathering point. Twist it together two times to secure it. Leave the long ends of the pipe cleaner hanging off to the sides. Your doll now has a head. The ends of the pipe cleaner are your doll's arms. The hanging end of the gathered tissue paper is its body.

5. Fold the ends of the pipe cleaner to give your doll hands.

6. Wrap a second pipe cleaner around the doll's waist. Twist it so it stays in place. Crisscross the two loose ends across the front of the doll's body and then around its neck. Twist the ends together twice at the front of your doll. If there is still extra pipe cleaner, curl it into a bow.

7. Pull the tissue paper apart at the bottom to create the doll's skirt.

8. Cut a piece of different colored tissue paper to measure 7 x 10 inches (18 x 25 cm). This will be your doll's hair. Fold the paper in half lengthwise. You should have a folded piece that is 3.5 x 10 inches (9 x 25 cm).

9. Cut two 2-inch (5 cm) pieces from a pipe cleaner.

10. Center the hairpiece on the top of your doll's head. Gather each side of the paper to form pigtails. Wrap the 2-inch (5 cm) pipe cleaner pieces around the gathered tissue paper to secure the pigtails.

11. Glue your doll's hair in place.

12. Give your doll eyes by gluing the sequins or googly eyes in place.

13. Draw a smile on your doll's face with a marker.

Stained Glass

If you've ever seen a stained glass window, you know how beautiful it can be when sunlight shines through bright colors. Try making your own stained glass decorations using tissue paper.

Materials

- Sketch paper
- Pencil
- Ruler
- Scissors
- 1 sheet of black construction paper
- Tissue paper (different colors)
- Clear contact paper

Steps

1. Think of a simple shape for your stained glass light catcher. For example, it could be an outline of an animal, a heart, a butterfly, or a flower. Draw the shape on your sketch paper. The sketch should be large enough to fill your black paper and leave a 1-inch (2.5 cm) border around the edge.

2. Cut the shape from your sketch paper and place it in the center of the sheet of black construction paper. Trace around the shape with your pencil.

3. Poke a hole in the middle of the traced shape and cut it out of the black construction paper. When you are finished, you should have an opening that matches your shape.

4. Carefully cut around the shape in your black paper, leaving a 1-inch (2.5 cm) border.

5. Cut up squares of your colored tissue paper. They can be small or large. Use many different colors.

6. Cut two pieces of contact paper that are larger than your black outline shape. They do not need to match the shape of your design. Lay one of the pieces of contact paper on the table, sticky side up.

7. Place your black outline shape in the middle of the contact paper.

8. Place the squares of tissue paper inside your cutout design. Fill the entire inside with tissue squares. Be careful to keep the tissue paper within the border of your design.

9. Place the second piece of contact paper over the entire thing, sticking all the pieces together. Press out any air bubbles.

10. Cut the excess contact paper away from the edges of your shape. Keep a ½-inch (1 cm) border.

11. You are now ready to tape your stained glass to the window. Tape it with the black border facing you. Admire your creation as it catches the sunlight!

Decoupage Flowerpot

Use tissue paper shapes to decoupage a flowerpot. Fill the flowerpot with paper carnations for a beautiful centerpiece.

Materials

- Old newspapers
- Glue
- Paper plate
- Pink or red tissue paper (a small piece)
- Terra-cotta flowerpot
- Paintbrushes (a 1-inch, or 2.5 cm, brush and a smaller craft brush)
- Yellow tissue paper
- Dark blue or green tissue paper
- Acrylic black paint
- Polycrylic
- Foam brush

Steps

1. Spread newspapers out to protect your work surface.
2. Carefully tear a small circle out of the pink or red tissue paper. This will be the center of your flower.
3. Pour the glue onto the paper plate. Use the 1-inch (2.5 cm) brush to paint glue onto the side of your pot and stick the flower center to the pot. Put more glue on top of it.

4. Tear petal shapes out of the yellow tissue paper. They do not need to be perfect because flowers in nature aren't always perfect!

5. Put more glue on your pot and decoupage the petals around the center of your flower.

6. Tear small pieces of the dark blue or green tissue paper. This will be your background color. Glue the dark pieces around the edges of your flower. You can shape your flower even more by covering the petal edges with the dark color. Once you have filled in the area around your flower, decoupage the dark color around the rest of the pot. Decoupage all the way to the top edge of your pot. Make the top edge as straight as you can. You do not need to decoupage the bottom of the pot.

7. Let the pot dry overnight.

8. Use the craft paintbrush to paint the top edge of your pot with a straight black line. Let the paint dry.

9. Use the foam brush to coat the entire outside of the pot with varnish. Let it dry. You are now ready to plant a flower in your pot. It also makes a nice pencil holder.

Candleholder

Decoupage a customized design onto a glass candleholder to create a colorful decoration for your room.

Materials

- Sketch paper
- Pencil
- Clear glass candleholder
- Tissue paper (different colors)
- Old newspapers
- Polycrylic
- Foam brush
- Gold leafing pen

Steps

1. Sketch ideas for the design you want to put on your candleholder. You can follow the design in this book or make up your own design.
2. Carefully clean and dry the glass candleholder.

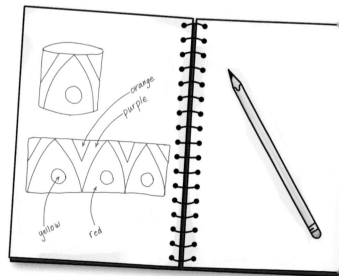

3. Cut or rip your tissue paper into the shapes you need for your design.

4. Spread newspapers out to protect your work surface.

5. Use your foam brush to add polycrylic to the spots on the candleholder where you want to stick the tissue paper. Stick the tissue to the glass and brush more polycrylic over the top.

6. Continue adding tissue paper to complete your candleholder. Did it turn out like your sketch?

7. Let the candleholder dry overnight. When it is dry, use the gold leafing pen to draw outlines around the paper shapes. Once the gold leaf is dry, you are ready to use the candleholder. Ask an adult to light the candle.

TIP
Candleholders make great presents!

Butterfly Mobile

Use tissue paper to create dozens of brightly colored butterflies. Hang them from a mobile for an eye-catching decoration.

Materials

- Tissue paper (different colors)
- Ruler
- Scissors
- Pencil
- Pipe cleaners
- Needle
- Embroidery thread
- Tree branch (about 2 feet, or 61 cm, long)

Steps

1. Cut 6 strips of different colored tissue paper. Each strip should measure 3 x 20 inches (8 x 51 cm).
2. Trace the butterfly pattern on the right onto one end of each strip of tissue paper.

3. Accordion fold each piece of tissue paper so that the butterfly shape remains on top. Make sure each section of folded paper is large enough to fit the entire butterfly pattern. Each fold will be about 3½ inches (9 cm).

4. With the strip folded, cut out the butterfly shape. Cut through all of the folded pieces of paper. You should get about seven butterfly shapes from each strip of paper.

5. Fold one of the pipe cleaners in half.

6. Place two different colored butterfly shapes together within the folded pipe cleaner. Gently twist the pipe cleaner to secure the tissue paper in place.

7. Curl and adjust the loose ends of pipe cleaner to make them look like antennae.

8. Gently pull the wings of the butterfly apart. The slight crinkle in the paper will make your butterfly look like it is flying.

9. Double thread your needle with 24 inches (61 cm) of thread. You should have a final thread length of 12 inches (30 cm).

10. Poke the needle between the folded pipe cleaner and the top layer of tissue. Before you pull the needle all the way through, guide the needle back through two strands of thread before the knot at the end. Once the needle is through, tighten the thread to the center of your butterfly's body. Cut the thread off at the needle.

11. Repeat steps 5 through 10 until you run out of butterfly shapes.

12. Tie the threads of your butterflies to the tree branch. Decorate the tree branch with as many butterflies as you like. The strings your butterflies hang from can be different lengths.

13. To hang your branch, tie a 24-inch (61 cm) piece of thread to one end of the branch. Tie the other end of the string to the other end of the branch.

14. Find the balancing point of your mobile by holding the middle of the string you just attached. Adjusting where you hold will change how your branch hangs. Once you find the place where the branch stays balanced, tie a 12-inch (30 cm) piece of thread at that point. Loop the thread around and tie the loose end to the center of where it is knotted to the balancing thread. Hang your mobile from the loop you created.

Keeping a Sketchbook Diary

As you have probably noticed while making some of the crafts in this book, sketch paper can be very helpful when planning your designs. Now that you have worked with tissue paper, you may have more ideas for future craft projects. Keeping a small sketchbook with you at all times can help you develop your ideas. Whenever inspiration strikes, grab your sketchbook and draw your ideas. Make notes to help you remember what you were thinking. Inventors and artists often keep notebooks by their bedsides just in case an idea comes in the middle of the night.

A sketchbook can also help you develop your old ideas into new ones. As you look over an idea, think about ways you can improve it. A simple idea can turn into an incredible project.

Glossary

diameter (dye-AM-i-tur) a straight line through the center of a circle, connecting opposite sides

industry (IN-duh-stree) a single branch of business or trade

tailor (TAY-lur) a person who makes or alters clothes

translucent (trans-LOO-suhnt) when a substance is not completely clear like glass but will let some light shine through

For More Information

Books

Ives, Rob. *Amazing Paper Pets: 6 Animated Animals to Make.* New York: Sterling Publishing Company, 2010.

McGee, Randel. *Paper Crafts for the 4th of July.* Berkeley Heights, NJ: Enslow Elementary, 2012.

Ruffler, Walter. *Paper Models That Move: 14 Ingenious Automata, and More.* Mineola, NY: Dover Publications, 2010.

Web Sites

Handmade Charlotte—6 Easy DIY Paper Party Decorations

www.handmadecharlotte.com/great-tissue-paper-diys-dont-involve-nose

Throwing a party? Visit this site for some ideas for decorating with tissue paper.

Spoonful—Fold & Fun! 25 Tissue Paper Crafts for Kids

http://spoonful.com/crafts/fun-tissue-paper-crafts-kids

Check out this Web site for more ideas for creations using tissue paper.

Index

About the Author

Kathleen Petelinsek is a children's book illustrator, writer, and designer. As a child, she spent her summers drawing and painting. She still loves to do the same today, but now all her work is done on the computer. When she isn't working on her computer, she can be found outside swimming, biking, running, or playing in the snow of southern Minnesota.